WE MOVE THE WORLD

WE MO
WO

To my kids, Dex and Delaney, who move my world every day—K.L.

For Ms. Lee, who inspired me to move the world—N.H.A.

Special thanks to Elise McMullen-Ciotti.

We Move the World • Text copyright © 2021 by Kari Lavelle • Illustrations copyright © 2021 by Nabigal-Nayagam Haider Ali
All rights reserved. Manufactured in Italy. • No part of this book may be used or reproduced in any manner whatsoever without
written permission except in the case of brief quotations embodied in critical articles and reviews. For information address
HarperCollins Children's Books, a division of HarperCollins Publishers, 195 Broadway, New York, NY 10007.
www.harpercollinschildrens.com • ISBN 978-0-06-291685-3 • The artist used Adobe Photoshop to create the digital illustrations
for this book. • Typography by Chelsea C. Donaldson • 21 22 23 24 25 RTLO 10 9 8 7 6 5 4 3 2 1 ❖ First Edition

VE THE RLD

by Kari Lavelle

pictures by Nabi H. Ali

HARPER

An Imprint of HarperCollins*Publishers*

First words and first steps—
we stretch;
we grow.
Reaching and climbing—
we wonder and play.
At home and school—
we stand up;
we show up.
In big and small ways,
we move the world.

We say our first words.
We use our voices for equality.

Supreme Court Justices Ruth Bader Ginsburg, Sonia Sotomayor, and
Elena Kagan have worked to ensure all are treated fairly under the law.

We take our first steps.
We walk on the moon.

Astronauts Buzz Aldrin and Neil Armstrong were
the first to step onto the surface of the moon, in 1969.

We stack blocks.
We build landmarks.

In 1886, courageous construction workers—many of whom were new immigrants—assembled the Statue of Liberty, an icon that continues to welcome travelers from all over the world.

We write the alphabet.
We blaze a trail with words.

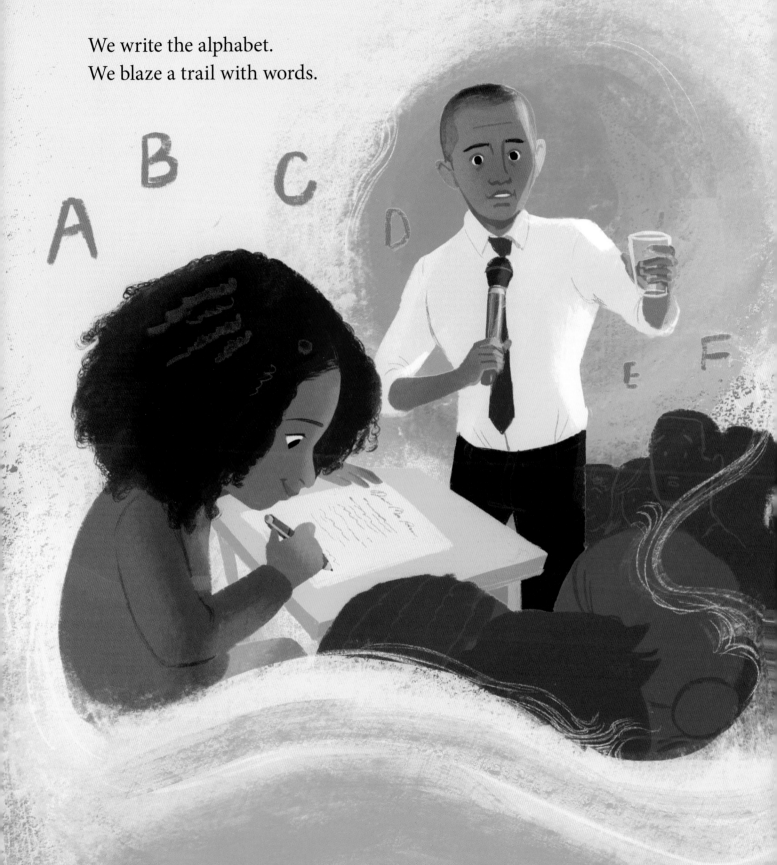

When eight-year-old Mari Copeny wrote to President Obama about the lead in her city's water, her letter gained his attention, and he made an official trip to Flint, Michigan. Americans learned about Flint's water problem and helped to get clean water for the people of Flint.

We jump in puddles.
We leap over obstacles.

Misty Copeland made history when she became the first African American principal ballerina in the American Ballet Theatre.

We sing our hearts out!
We unite our voices in harmony.

On one night in 1985, dozens of famous singers came together to record the song "We Are the World," which raised over $60 million to help fix the growing hunger problem in Africa.

We draw a picture all by ourselves.
We create a memorial with others.

First displayed in 1987,
the AIDS Memorial Quilt
honors the thirty-two
million lives that have been
lost to HIV/AIDS.

We soar into the sky!
We take flight with our inventions!

The Wright brothers became the first to design,
build, and successfully pilot an airplane, in 1903.

We conquer the monkey bars.
We win Olympic medals!

Oksana Masters has won gold, silver, and bronze medals in skiing,
rowing, cycling, and biathlon events at the Paralympics.

We search for seashells on the shore.
We dive deep to expand our world.

Sylvia Earle walked on the ocean floor at the deepest depths anyone ever had and set the world record in 1979.

We share with friends.
We encourage kindness.

Fred Rogers started the television
program *Mister Rogers' Neighborhood* for
children in 1968. Decades later, his vision
for compassion continues.

We plant flowers.
We sow the seeds for change.

Wangari Maathai founded the
Green Belt Movement in 1977, an
organization that planted thirty
million trees!

We solve puzzles.
We hold the key.

Native American code talkers were critical in both World Wars, the Korean War, and the Vietnam War because they used their own Indigenous languages to communicate secret messages to Allied troops, saving thousands of lives.

We take a knee for an injured player.
We kneel for social justice.

In 2016, as thousands anticipated the game in the stadium and millions more watched on their televisions at home, Colin Kaepernick kneeled during the national anthem to protest how Black people are treated in the United States.

We cheer for our friends!
We march for love.

There are LGBTQ+ Pride parades all around the world.
In 2017, in São Paulo, Brazil, over five million people
showed up to celebrate the right to choose who to love.

We care for others.
We rescue our community.

Spending all day on their feet and risking their own lives, healthcare workers treated patients during the coronavirus pandemic that began in 2020.

We stand up to bullies.
We speak up to speak out.

At seventeen years old, Malala Yousafzai became the youngest winner of the Nobel Peace Prize for her work in advocating education for Pakistani girls.

We dream about our future.
We rise up for a better world.

On a hot day in 1963, people came from all over the country to hear Dr. Martin Luther King Jr. speak his now-famous words "I have a dream . . ."

As movers and shakers,
   we inquire;
   we inspire.
As artists and activists,
   we persist;
   we resist.
As dreamers and doers,
   we believe;
   we achieve.
How you move just might
MOVE THE WORLD!

TIMELINE

1886: The Statue of Liberty is assembled.

1903: The Wright brothers successfully fly the first airplane.

1963: Dr. Martin Luther King Jr. speaks at the March on Washington for Jobs and Freedom.

1968: *Mister Rogers' Neighborhood* makes its national debut on public television.

1969: Buzz Aldrin and Neil Armstrong land on the moon.

1970: The first LGBTQ+ Pride parades take place in New York City, San Francisco, Los Angeles, and Chicago.

1979: Sylvia Earle becomes the first person to walk on the bottom of the ocean, wearing the diving suit Jim.

1981: Sandra Day O'Connor is appointed to the U.S. Supreme Court.

1985: The song "We Are the World" is recorded.

1987: The AIDS quilt is first displayed at the National Mall in Washington, DC.

1993: Ruth Bader Ginsburg is appointed to the U.S. Supreme Court.

2004: Wangari Maathai wins the Nobel Peace Prize for her work with the Green Belt Movement.

2009: Sonia Sotomayor is sworn in as the 111th justice of the Supreme Court.

2010: Elena Kagan is appointed to the U.S. Supreme Court.

2012: Oksana Masters competed in her first Paralympics, winning a bronze medal in rowing.

2014: Malala Yousafzai wins the Nobel Peace Prize for her work advocating education for women.

2015: Misty Copeland becomes the first African American principal ballerina of the American Ballet Theatre.

2016: Mari Copeny writes a letter to President Obama about the water in Flint, Michigan.

2016: Colin Kaepernick kneels during the national anthem to protest how Black people are treated.

2020–: COVID-19 affects millions of people around the world.

NOTES ABOUT THE EVENTS

WOMEN ON THE SUPREME COURT

Elena Kagan, Sonia Sotomayor, and Ruth Bader Ginsburg have changed the world by serving on the Supreme Court, deciding if laws are fair and just for all. Since the establishment of the Supreme Court in 1790, only 4 justices (out of 114!) have been women. The first woman appointed to the Supreme Court was Sandra Day O'Connor in 1981. Ruth Bader Ginsburg was the first Jewish woman appointed as associate justice, and Sonia Sotomayor was the first Latina appointed. Before her appointment as an associate justice of the Supreme Court, attorney Ruth Bader Ginsburg fought for equal treatment of women in her first case before the Supreme Court—and she won!

FIRST WALK ON THE MOON

On July 16, 1969, Buzz Aldrin, Neil Armstrong, and Michael Collins climbed aboard Apollo 11 and lifted off from Kennedy Space Center. Four days later, they approached the moon. Collins orbited the moon while Aldrin and Armstrong piloted the Eagle Lunar Module to the surface. With just seconds to spare before they would have to abort their mission due to low fuel, they landed on the moon, announcing "the Eagle has landed" to Mission Control Center in Houston 240,000 miles away. Aldrin and Armstrong explored the moon for two hours before they made their return flight to Earth. When news broke of their successful mission, people all around the world believed that anything was possible.

"One small step for [a] man, one giant leap for mankind."

THE STATUE OF LIBERTY

The Statue of Liberty construction crews built the 151-foot-high, 450,000-pound (that's about 157 cars!) statue from 214 crates shipped from France. When the statue was completed, she had a brown appearance from the copper material used, but over time the copper shell oxidized to become the blue-green color it is now. As the official name "Liberty Enlightening the World" implies, the Statue of Liberty is more than a landmark. She is a portal to a new world and a symbol of friendship between the United States and France. The broken shackles at her feet symbolize independence and freedom from oppression. Her torch symbolically lights the way to liberty and freedom. She stands for hope and opportunity.

"Give me your tired, your poor,
Your huddled masses yearning to breathe free,
The wretched refuse of your teeming shore.
Send these, the homeless, tempest-tost to me,
I lift my lamp beside the golden door!"
  —Emma Lazarus

MARI COPENY

Amariyanna "Mari" Copeny's activism started at a young age. At eight years old, "Little Miss Flint" knew it was unlikely that her letter to President Obama about Flint's unsafe water would be read by him, but she wrote it anyway. President Obama not only read Mari's letter, but he also made an official trip to Flint and allocated $100 million to improve the city's water system. Mari uses her voice to improve her community and empower other kids to do the same.

"[President Obama's] trip proved to me that a kid can change the world."

MISTY COPELAND

Misty Copeland first put on ballet shoes when she was thirteen years old. For the first two weeks of class, she just watched, too nervous to participate, but it wasn't long before she fell in love with ballet. When her family had to move, Misty stayed with her dance teacher so she could continue ballet instruction. Years later, when Misty earned a spot at the American Ballet Theatre, she was the only African American dancer in the corps de ballet. Her hard work paid off when she became the first African American principal ballerina for ABT in 2015.

"Decide what you want. Declare it to the world. See yourself winning. And remember that if you are persistent as well as patient, you can get whatever you seek."

"WE ARE THE WORLD"

The USA for Africa project originated with the song's writers, Lionel Richie and Michael Jackson, and its producer, Quincy Jones. After the American Music Awards in 1985, forty-six vocalists, including Willie Nelson, Tina Turner, Stevie Wonder, Diana Ross, Bob Dylan, and Bruce Springsteen, stayed up all night (they finished at 8:00 a.m.!) to record the song. "We Are the World" raised $63 million as well as awareness to the hunger problem in Africa.

"We are the world
We are the children
We are the ones who make a brighter day, so let's start giving."

AIDS MEMORIAL QUILT

The NAMES Project Foundation first displayed the AIDS quilt in 1987 at the National Mall in Washington, DC. The quilt, composed of 1,920 panels, was larger than a football field. Now it has over 48,000 panels and is the largest community art project in the world. Each panel honors the life of a loved one—a friend, parent, relative, husband, or wife. Famous civil rights activist Rosa Parks created a panel for her friend Deborah. People in thirty-five countries have contributed panels. The AIDS quilt continues to tour the world, raising money, promoting awareness, inspiring others, and memorializing the lives of those lost to the AIDS epidemic.

THE WRIGHT BROTHERS

It all started with a present from Orville and Wilbur's father, a flying toy made of rubber bands and wood. The brothers' curiosity led them to their own toy and bicycle designs. Soon their interest turned to flying machines. In 1899, they made a glider. Then they added an engine and propellers. The brothers traveled from their home in Ohio to windy Kitty Hawk, North Carolina, to test their invention. On December 17, 1903, Orville flew 120 feet for 12 seconds. Their invention worked! On their fourth attempt, the plane traveled 852 feet over 59 seconds. In 1909, Wilbur flew a plane around the Statue of Liberty while a million people watched from below. Six decades later, Neil Armstrong was so inspired by the Wright brothers' aeronautical feat that he brought a small piece of their plane as a memento on Apollo 11's lunar journey.

OKSANA MASTERS

Newly adopted from a Ukrainian orphanage, seven-year-old Oksana Masters was determined to get across the monkey bars and she wasn't going to let the fact that she was born without thumbs get in her way! Oksana was born with extra toes and webbed hands, and both of her legs had to be amputated. Even though her disabilities presented more challenges as she got older, her competitive spirit and athleticism led her to success as an athlete. At thirteen, she learned how to row and has been competing in sports ever since. She won a bronze medal in her first Paralympics in 2012. Her grit and determination inspire others. Her performances at the Paralympics make Team USA proud!

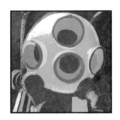

SYLVIA EARLE

Growing up on a farm in New Jersey, young Sylvia Earle loved exploring the nature that surrounded her. She fell in love with the ocean at twelve years old when her family moved to beachside Florida. Her natural interests steered her toward a career in research as an oceanographer. In 1979, in Hawaii, using a special diving suit called Jim, Sylvia was the first person to walk on the bottom of the ocean solo and untethered, 1,250 feet below the surface. Sylvia continues to advocate for the protection of ocean ecosystems.

FRED ROGERS

Mister Rogers' Neighborhood made its national broadcast debut in 1968 with educational programming that encouraged the expression of feelings and addressed difficult topics directly. The show was known for Fred Rogers' signature cardigan sweaters (his mother knit him a new one each year!), his ritual of taking off his shoes, traveling to the Neighborhood of Make-Believe, and the many friends on the show: Lady Aberlin, Officer Clemmons, X the Owl, and Daniel Tiger. Some shows had guest appearances, including oceanographer Sylvia Earle, who snorkeled with Mr. Rogers and discussed ocean life. Thirty years and 895 episodes later, the legacy of this show remains. Fred Rogers Productions continues to create programming that targets the whole child: *Peg + Cat*, *The Odd Squad*, and *Daniel Tiger's Neighborhood*, named after the original puppet from the Mister Rogers show.

When tragedies strike, we still look to his words for guidance and comfort.

"When I was a boy and I would see scary things in the news, my mother would say to me, 'Look for the helpers. You will always find people who are helping.'"

WANGARI MAATHAI

Wangari Maathai was disheartened by the deforestation she observed in her native Kenya. So in 1977, she started planting seedlings. She encouraged local women to do the same by paying them to plant trees. Although her ideas were peaceful in nature, Wangari was criticized and even arrested several times for her work. By 2004, Mama Miti, which means "the mother of trees," and her Green Belt Movement had increased the income of eighty thousand people and planted thirty million trees, affecting positive change in thirty countries in Africa. Planting trees prevents soil erosion, provides food, firewood, and shelter, and filters air and water. Wangari's work empowered women, changed the ecology of Kenya, and earned her the Nobel Peace Prize in 2004 (the first African woman to win the award).

"To the young people I say, you are a gift to your communities and indeed the world. You are our hope and our future."

NATIVE AMERICAN CODE TALKERS

In 1918, during World War I, the Germans had cracked all of the codes American troops used to send messages. But when the U.S. military began using Choctaw soldiers to send messages using their own language in coded forms, the enemy was unable to decode them, making a difference in the battles in France and helping to end the war sooner.

At the time, Indigenous people within the United States were not considered U.S. citizens, yet some felt compelled to join the Allied war effort. Eventually, Congress granted Native Americans U.S. citizenship in 1924, although some states withheld their rights until 1948.

When World War II broke out, the U.S. successfully relied on code talkers to send messages since they were more efficient than other coding methods, including coding machines. While the most famous code talkers were Navajo, Comanche, and Sioux, U.S. military communications utilized around twenty coded forms of Indigenous languages from over thirty Native Nations. Code talkers gave Allied forces the advantage, ending the wars earlier and with victory.

COLIN KAEPERNICK

As the national anthem played before the San Francisco 49ers–San Diego Chargers game in 2016, Colin Kaepernick kneeled to protest the treatment of Black people by police officers. Some people disagreed with him and booed him. Others were inspired and showed their support. Some athletes, like soccer player Megan Rapinoe, started to kneel too. His actions moved people to start conversations about how to make changes.

LGBTQ+ PRIDE PARADE

The first LGBTQ+ Pride parades took place in Chicago, San Francisco, Los Angeles, and New York City in 1970, one year after the Stonewall Riots. Now Pride parades take place in cities all over the world. People celebrate the right to choose who to love by dressing colorfully and expressing themselves. São Paulo, Brazil, hosts one of the biggest Pride parades in the world, with millions of people in attendance.

COVID-19 HEALTHCARE WORKERS

Begining in 2020, the spread of the (SARS-CoV-2) coronavirus caused schools, churches, and businesses to close. The virus infected millions of people around the world. Doctors and nurses tirelessly helped those who were sick. Most people recovered from the COVID-19 disease, but many did not. Healthcare and essential workers put their own lives at risk every day when they went to work.

MALALA YOUSAFZAI

Malala Yousafzai grew up in a household that valued her education. Her father ran his own school and was a respected community leader. However, in Pakistan, women did not have the same rights as men. Malala had to attend school secretly. Even when the Taliban tried to silence Malala through threats and physical violence, she continued to speak out for education for girls. Malala won the Nobel Peace Prize when she was seventeen years old, the youngest recipient ever. She continues to use her voice to empower women and fight for their opportunities.

"One child, one teacher, one pen, one book can change the world."

DR. MARTIN LUTHER KING JR.

Dr. Martin Luther King Jr. worked on his speech until 4:00 a.m. the night before the 1963 March on Washington for Jobs and Freedom. He wanted to say the right words for the 250,000 people attending the event. The next day, Dr. King started with his prepared speech. But when gospel singer Mahalia Jackson shouted, "Tell them about the dream, Martin!" he abandoned his written speech and spontaneously went on to express some of the most famous and inspiring words ever spoken.

"I have a dream that my four little children will one day live in a nation where they will not be judged by the color of their skin but by the content of their character."

SELECTED BIBLIOGRAPHY

WOMEN ON THE SUPREME COURT
Levy, Debbie, illustrated by Elizabeth Baddeley. *I Dissent: Ruth Bader Ginsburg Makes Her Mark*. Simon & Schuster, 2016.
Sotomayor, Sonia, illustrated by Lulu Delacre. *Turning Pages: My Life Story*. Philomel Books, 2018.
www.supremecourt.gov

FIRST WALK ON THE MOON
Aldrin, Buzz, illustrated by Wendell Minor. *Buzz Aldrin: Reaching for the Moon*. HarperCollins, 2005.
Floca, Brian. *Moonshot: The Flight of Apollo 11*. Atheneum Books for Young Readers, 2019.
Greene, Rhonda Gowler, illustrated by Scott Brundage. *The First Men Who Went to the Moon*. Sleeping Bear Press, 2019.

THE STATUE OF LIBERTY
Byrd, Robert. *Liberty Arrives! How America's Grandest Statue Found Her Home*. Dial Books for Young Readers, 2019.
Eggers, Dave, illustrated by Shawn Harris. *Her Right Foot*. Chronicle Books, 2017.

MARI COPENY
Lowry, Mary Pauline. "This Is How One Sixth Grade Girl Helped Improve Flint's Water Crisis." *The Oprah Magazine*, 17 Dec. 2018.
www.maricopeny.com

MISTY COPELAND
Copeland, Misty. *Life in Motion: An Unlikely Ballerina [Young Reader's Edition]*. Aladdin, 2016.
Copeland, Misty, and Christopher Myers. *Firebird*. Putnam, 2014.

"WE ARE THE WORLD"
www.songfacts.com/facts/usa-for-africa/we-are-the-world
www.usaforafrica.org

AIDS MEMORIAL QUILT
Atkins, Jeannine, illustrated by Tad Hills. *A Name on the Quilt: A Story of Remembrance*. Aladdin, 2003.
Jones, Cleve, and Jeff Dawson. *Stitching a Revolution: The Making of an Activist*. HarperCollins World, 2000.
www.aidsquilt.org

THE WRIGHT BROTHERS
Buckley, James, illustrated by Tim Foley. *Who Were the Wright Brothers?* Grosset & Dunlap, 2014.
Jenner, Caryn. *First Flight: The Story of the Wright Brothers*. DK Publishing, 2003.

OKSANA MASTERS
www.oksanamastersusa.com
www.paralympic.org

& FURTHER RESOURCES

SYLVIA EARLE
Earle, Sylvia A. *Dive!: My Adventures in the Deep Frontier*. National Geographic Society, 1999.
Nivola, Claire A. *Life in the Ocean: The Story of Sylvia Earle*. Frances Foster Books, 2012.
www.mission-blue.org

FRED ROGERS
Bailey, Diane. *Who Was Mister Rogers?* Penguin Workshop, 2019.
Rogers, Fred, illustrated by Luke Flowers. *A Beautiful Day in the Neighborhood: The Poetry of Mister Rogers*. Quirk Books, 2019.

WANGARI MAATHAI
Napoli, Donna Jo, illustrated by Kadir Nelson. *Mama Miti: Wangari Maathai and the Trees of Kenya*. Simon & Schuster Books for Young Readers, 2010.
Prévot, Franck, illustrated by Aurélia Fronty. *Wangari Maathai: The Woman Who Planted Millions of Trees*. Charlesbridge, 2015.
www.greenbeltmovement.org

NATIVE AMERICAN CODE TALKERS
Bruchac, Joseph, illustrated by Liz Amini-Holmes. *Chester Nez and the Unbreakable Code: A Navajo Code Talker's Story*. Albert Whitman & Company, 2018.
Dennis, Elizabeth, illustrated by Valerio Fabbretti. *Fearless Flyers, Dazzle Painters, and Code Talkers! World War I*. Simon Spotlight, 2018.

COLIN KAEPERNICK
Watson, Stephanie. *Colin Kaepernick*. Capstone Press, a Capstone Imprint, 2019.

LGBTQ+ PRIDE PARADE
Pitman, Gayle E., illustrated by Kristina Litten. *This Day in June*. Magination Press, 2014.
www.history.com/news/how-activists-plotted-the-first-gay-pride-parades

COVID-19 HEALTHCARE WORKERS
www.nytimes.com/interactive/2020/world/coronavirus-health-care-workers.html

MALALA YOUSAFZAI
Maslo, Lina. *Free as a Bird: The Story of Malala*. Balzer + Bray, 2018.
Yousafzai, Malala, and Patricia McCormick. *Malala: My Story of Standing Up for Girls' Rights*. Little, Brown and Company, 2018.

DR. MARTIN LUTHER KING JR.
Farris, Christine King, illustrated by London Ladd. *March On! The Day My Brother Martin Changed the World*. Scholastic Press, 2008.
King, Dr. Martin Luther, Jr., illustrated by Kadir Nelson. *I Have a Dream: Dr. Martin Luther King, Jr.* Schwartz & Wade Books, 2012.
Wittenstein, Barry, illustrated by Jerry Pinkney. *A Place to Land*. Neal Porter Books, 2019.